L U N C H

lunch

BY D. A. POWELL

Wesleyan University Press
Published by University Press of New England   ·   Hanover and London

Wesleyan University Press

Published by University Press of New England, Hanover, NH 03755

Printed in the United States of America

5 4 3 2 1

CIP data appear at the end of the book

Portions of this manuscript have appeared, perhaps in a slightly different form, in the following pub-

lications: *Prairie Schooner, Denver Quarterly, New American Writing, Northeast Journal, Iowa Review, Iowa Journal of*

Cultural Studies, James White Review, Pleiades, Pequod, Explosive, Boomerang, Jejune, 33 Review, Fence, Lilliput Review,

Fishdrum, Lost & Found Times, Boston Review, Carbuncle, Experimental Basement, In Tense, Chiron Review, Antenym, and

Puerto del Sol; and in the following anthologies: *The World In Us* (St. Martin's Press), *Word of Mouth* (Talis-

man House), and *Imperfect Paradise* (University of Southern Illinois Press). "[triptych]" was included in

the chapbook *explosions and small geometries* (Norton Coker Press, 1991).

My thanks to the James Michener Foundation, for a Paul Engel Fellowship, which afforded me the

time to work on this book.

And thanks once more to the angels who read this work when it was in development and who of-

fered advice: David Bromige, Carol Ciavonne, Patricia Hartnett, Sam Witt, John Isles, Rachel Zucker,

Tom Thompson, Alec Dinwoodie, Ryan Berg.

"All night. All day. The angels keep watching over me."

for Kirk Fruehling

"At last we had let them speak, the children whom flowers had made statues

For the rivers of water which came from their funnel;

And we stood there in the middle of existence

Dazzled by the white paraffin of lunch. "

—Kenneth Koch, "Lunch"

CONTENTS

[second fugue]   6

SOFTLY AND TENDERLY   7

[of all the modern divisions: time splits]   8
[maybe he wears my trousers: lagniappe]   9
[triptych]   10
[studs and rings: favors of the piercing party]   11
[he pleasures me: a nasty flick. quiescent]   12
[slashed his foot as a boy. heel to toe]   13
[the mind is a shapely genital. faces: elaborate]   14
[personal]   15
[a conch: I washed ashore on more than one atoll]   16
[my father and me making dresses: together]   17
[my father and me in hollywood: fading and rising starlets] 18
[my fingers have performed their services: church steeple people] 19

SWEET BY AND BY   20

[simple endings overlap: grief is interference]   21
[the sad part of living is eating and dying]   22
[sounding the depths: she slides into the bath]   23
[attended by miracles. every man has two angels]   24

[sheet wrapped as a burnoose. about his head]   25

[the agricultural application of burial]   26

[your torso: enticing to insects. like me]   27

[remembering the taste of skin: dim prehistory of dives]   28

[choose equal weights: berries and sugar]   29

[the minotaur at supper: spare the noritake and the spode]   30

[darling can you kill me: with your mickeymouse pillows]   31

[thinking the think that falls away: my soul he has no hours to waste]   32

[you're thin again handsome. in our last]   33

GATHER AT THE RIVER   34

[always returning: holidays and burials. not every week]   35

[not the treats of quince blossoms. in this rainy cycle the yards]   36

[autumn set us heavily to task: unrooted the dahlias]   37

[splat in the oatmeal: granddaddy facedown]   38

[here comes the welcome wagon with its]   39

[women stitching apron corners together. neighborly]   40

[the future rose: an a-frame on the cumberland]   41

[splitzville for ann and mark: the tourniquet]   42

[he achieved his escape: john wesley]   43

[orphans of career day: the choicest lives already]   44

[down with the chickenbumps you came: kerplunk]   45

[he imitates his wife: no young drop from the gap]   46

[dearest perdition. your sweet peach kisses lost]   47

[baby's on a pallet. in the screenporch you iron]   48

[sonnet]   49

[the rain deliberately falls: as an older boy's hand]   50

[old age keeps its reservation. nostalgia]   51

IN THE MIDDLE OF THE AIR   52

[we all carry signs of our obsessions]   53

[third-world hunger strikes you. midtown bus]   54

[in the new genesis: a part of his skeleton became me. shaped me]   55

[you don't have syphilis. the doctor says]   56

[because as lives are aching I am lucky: a poisonal cup]   57

[in the course of travel: strychnine every few hours. some italian art]   58

[when dementia begins: almost makes sense like hamburger translations]   59

[cherry elixir: the first medication. so mary poppins]   60

LUNCH

[second fugue]

a poisonal cup: they can tell that their little boy is lonesome which he is

lifting belly seeks pleasure: in this position.

                                                 of wishing between his thighs

I must say grace over his thighs.   if you know how to say *pansy* say *pansies*

certainly some said this of him.   you still can hear them:

                                                           spreading a blanket

even the telling   [which might annoy them does annoy them]

                                                 alas a dirty word

and not *annoy*: *anoint*.   anneal this rude flesh with balm and aloes

lilies.   sorghum and sour apples barely keep him: lily wet lily wet while

one taste one tack, one taste one bottle.   an infant dose. *sleep*

                                                 on the nightstand

no more doves can land here.   the pigeon on the grass alas

                                     and the magpie in the sky

expect to rest just as well.   a second coming:

                                     when this you see remember

*c[?]nt how poems
come to us?*

                              I

softly and tenderly

"I have been to lots of parties

and acted perfectly disgraceful

but I never actually collapsed

oh Lana Turner we love you get up"

—Frank O'Hara, "Poem"

[of all the modern divisions: time splits]

of all the modern divisions: time splits

you are the one: lunch

egalitarian in your traverseability

more than embargoes or frontiers or zippers

can torture with visible boundaries

you invite [spreading a blanket] to be taken

kissed reverently upon the lips

may not always have you.   but we've had you

taken mementos.   hurried away to engage

a dull career.   meet you secretly.   on the side

[maybe he wears my trousers: lagniappe]

maybe he wears my trousers: lagniappe

he is the same age as my memory of him.   leaning

into the menial wage.   the pockets tattered

sorghum and sour apples barely keep him

bony: an architecture of tentposts.   supporting

constellations.   the points where light

enters: frayed patches.   weakening seams

Williams
meets
Crane

[triptych]

once   we kissed   the world

goodbye   aware   that it

was dying   of all   contained

within   these lines   I'll keep

two breaths   and you   to one side

of me   laughing   on the nightstand

[studs and rings: favors of the piercing party]

". . . and so he dug a hole deep in the ground,

and went and whispered in it what kind of ears King Midas had."

—Ovid

studs and rings: favors of the piercing party

hole in the head.   you got your rightwrongright ear

sent out in a press release: post self disclosure

boys admired your jewels.   for a time

you liked getting stuck.   and advertised

when did you close your legs: no openings

available you whisper like a tease.   but rumors

trail behind you in the reeds: "golden boy

has suggestive ears."   you still can hear them

—for *Alec Anderson*

8

[he pleasures me: a nasty flick. quiescent]

he pleasures me: a nasty flick.   quiescent
the still of him.   we set a long exposure

frame by frame: no candid voice over: the eye
so easily deceived requests a replay: how

many times the act can be performed
slo mo.   po mo.   ho mo.   iris into a field of blue

[slashed his foot as a boy. heel to toe]

slashed his foot as a boy.   heel to toe
on the living coral.   attempted to cure the sore
in a mortal swabbing: iodine

catalyst: pink branches of exo-skeleton
informed the soft canvas of limbs

mollusks were pried from his barrier.   feeding
frenzy of sharks at the jagged perimeter

polyps grown into a reef.   trawling ships
keep the distance.   he sings their sails away

[the mind is a shapely genital. faces: elaborate]

the mind is a shapely genital.   faces: elaborate

fig leaves.   disturbed by occasional gusts

modesty muh-dear.   admits impediment.   I don't

mind saying: like you better with your clothes

off.   but sober and with all your wits about

line break = potential energy?
tension?

[personal]

HETERO LIFE WANTED: me to move in.   share

a double entendre.   2 fireplaces and a kid

spacious: a must see.   soon I'd be having my eggs

poached.   because that's the way I would like them

toast: cut to triangles.   napkins: folded to hats

but could we stand to grow up together.   learn

ABC's and respectable manners.   would I have to shake hands

with the guy pals: firm.   longing for the visegrip of thighs

12

[a conch: I washed ashore on more than one atoll]

a conch: I washed ashore on more than one atoll

no shipwrecked soul traced my steps.   archipelago

of private beaches.   I sought no rescue from maroon

yare sloops would nestle in my coves: come

to suck hermetic creatures from their shells.   girls

opened sweet blossoms for me: boys rubbed firm

nipples into my back.   buried me head in the sand

a youngster lashes himself to a raft.   classic

romance.   catches the drift: especially away

possibility

have him veer

metaphor

proud of

—artifice

[my father and me making dresses: together]

my father and me making dresses: together
we debutantes.   cruel in lace bodices

we swoon to saxophones and rich husbands.   late
afternoon: shots of brandy in our cocoa

aren't I blessed with a young father firm
and flouncy: giggling in his petticoats

the other boys sigh when he mows the lawn
they fumble with their pockets and blush

while we two chums.   in a workshop of taffeta
never tire of chat: rugby or crushes or appliqué

I put my knee in his back.   I cinch and cinch
as preparing for an antebellum barbeque

where an ashley longworth could be filled with regret
and atlanta explode its host of scarlet poppies

[my father and me in hollywood: fading and rising starlets]

my father and me in hollywood: fading and rising starlets
look at me as sandra dee.   and he: the drugstore lana turner

how life imitates "imitation of life."   we were of two minds

the actress and her actress daughter mirror the actress/daughter
dynamic of the father/son mother/daughter charade

I tweedled as dumb as sandra dee was.   and as sandra dum
doted on daddy I doted on daddy's boyfriend.   and daddy

that has-been with his porcelana skin creme and his mafioso
brought out the bitter lezzie in me.   oh: as in "we were white."

but he could have been the patient dark-skinned housekeeper
a cut above a mammy mommy dearest daddy.   and I
the bitchy high yellow ungrateful child who passed as easily
as white.   as I was a white black child actress anywho

at the end of my father.   the end of the hollywood star
at the end of the fifties.   at the end of beauty itself

I cast myself as myself on his/her casket while mahalia
jackson sang sweet swing low sweet cheryl crane
sandra dee daughter/son black & white technicolor refrains.   oh sweet
mommy/daddy oh poor porcelana turner I love you.   get up

—for Peter Gizzi

[my fingers have performed their services: church steeple people]

jo (Scottish): sweetheart (pl. joes)

JO (Queer): jack-off

my fingers have performed their services: church steeple people

all bald.   all slender: the chapped rafters where a prayer echoes

have congregated round me.   clamored to be baptised

in the name of some daddy.   some boy.   some holy ghost

I have allowed this decalogue dominion: census takers

who tally by heads.   cradle me stealthily as mary and st. jos.

[patron of families.   confectioners.   and funeral directors]

and take me after a passion: anneal this rude flesh with balm and aloes *rep.*

I have counted upon their strokes to uncrypt the dead.   *supernature*

to shatter the snowy vessel [rosebud]   where the eye's light slows

these ten have been my lovers: callous.   constant and inconstant

in their bad disguises.   flicker of trick-or-treaters in my bedclothes

pinky to thumb I count their names: kevin, danny, cliff, ernie, kenny, , , , ,

the jeffs close in to me.   the joes.   and [curving and bending] the joes

experience + alters language?
perception

16

sweet by and by

"Think of him, the one you loved, on his knees, on his elbows, his face turned up to look back in yours, his mouth dark in his dark beard. He was smiling because of you"

—Allen Barnett, *The Body and Its Dangers*

[simple endings overlap: grief is interference]

simple endings overlap: grief is interference

we don't call dead air by the sound it makes

a scratching of monkey's paw disrupts stillness

life is a poor edit.   clip cut and paste

journal of caducity: no entry yet under "I"

too young to have amassed this catalogue.   obits

collected butterfly wings.   clippings of a summer lawn

an unsayable?
leads to emotional
potency

[the sad part of living is eating and dying]

the sad part of living is eating and dying
our dialogue breaks off mid-sentence

the bill arrives as a eulogy: itemized
everyone swallows a breathmint.   repression

nevermind the cost: I'll pick up your tab
you got the cab.   these days green and folding

[sounding the depths: she slides into the bath]

sounding the depths: she slides into the bath

displacement: acres of her frame bob as tiny azores

promontory of a neck above the diluvian world

why the tendency to represent ship as woman: buoyant

she is born from the sea.   anemone in its element

civilizations ended one drop at a time.   she held them

under: lost continents.   eventually the floods must subside

land is sighted: a new atlantis?   yawning the whirlpool widens

—for "Mother" Press Fulcher

[attended by miracles. every man has two angels]

a song of the apocrypha

attended by miracles.   every man has two angels
on duty.   how the divisions of hell quarrel
in the world to come: who shall be cast out

a bewitched young man: christ rises again
circumcised in the cave.   an idol falls
his death demanded to order in the church

we must fear god: militant and lying
christ at play makes a dead boy speak.   what
rules are given for this purpose: to suffer

[sheet wrapped as a burnoose. about his head]

sheet wrapped as a burnoose.   about his head
tubes fill his mouth with opium: diversions

keep him occupied: a palestine whose defenses
are suppressed.   territory lost.   frail arms
impuissant: his sky is a rattling dry gourd

here is a man from a country without borders
anyone can cross over: share his bed.   lazaretto

[the agricultural application of burial]

the agricultural application of burial
you're laying the lawn: a poultice roots
into the gash you cut in the ground

kenny.   service here is terrible
no decent waiting upon: cold picnic
over your salad memorial.   gnawed bones

I want to peel back the grass like bandages
just as I lift these corners.   shaking crumbs

multipliaty

[your torso: enticing to insects. like me]

your torso: enticing to insects.   like me

they want to bug you.   bugger you.   cocoons

pupate in those buttocks of adobe: anthills

untimely your nectar draws me: bouquet

exchanged for a pinwheel.   the foiled sentinel

over the stone sayonara which brailles itself

as a curious welcome mat: you took it for a hat

webs are your veil: tumulus beetles the maids

scramble to catch those spikenards.   a demimonde

by whom you are compromised.   in this position

imagination might have wedded us.   to share

[remembering the taste of skin: dim prehistory of dives]

remembering the taste of skin: dim prehistory of dives

secretions of the body: spume and seawater
cells of the voluble tongue welcome old chums

rapture of the deep: lungs fill with oceania
rubber suit flops into the skiff.   fins in the water

[choose equal weights: berries and sugar]

a song of Alice B. Toklas

choose equal weights: berries and sugar
a someone with influence.   likely to judge
twelve hours of maceration: skim and boil

any devoted friend might cook dishes
other than sweet ones.   august insupportable
and blisteringly hot yields little

jelly is ardently desired: simplest
or quickest to make.   remove from flame
and cool.   lest its delicacy should sour

[the minotaur at supper: spare the noritake and the spode]

the minotaur at supper: spare the noritake and the spode
from these ungular hands.   goblet stems scattered at my hoofs

a spattering of color on my hide.   remnants of one youth
another impaled on my horns: I must say grace over his thighs
for there may be no path back to him.   the way is dim and twists

myself am halfboy.   am beauty and the end of same: a hungry thing
hunts me also: through which passageway do my nostrils sense blood
what aperture brings me air salted with cries of the ancient corrida

metaphor
vo persona

28

[darling can you kill me: with your mickeymouse pillows]

darling can you kill me: with your mickeymouse pillows
when I'm a meager man.   with your exhaust pipe and hose

could you put me out: when I'm a mite a splinter a grain
a tatter a snip a sliver a whit a tittle.   habited by pain

would you bop me on the noggin: with a two by four
the trifle of me pissing myself.   slobbering infantile: or

wheezing in an oxygen tent.   won't you shut off the tank
mightn't you disconnect the plug: give the cord a proper yank

when I lose the feeling in my legs.   when my hands won't grip
and I'm a thread a reed a wrack a ruin: of clap and flux and grippe

with your smack connections could you dose me.   as I start my decline
would you put a bullet through me.   angel: no light left that is mine

—for Sam Witt

29

[thinking the think that falls away: my soul he has no hours to waste]

thinking the think that falls away: my soul he has no hours to waste

but is a wasting word.   wonderful sport in losing.   *sere* and *wear* and *dree*

why would I want time now?

                              as if enduring a ragtag second of the galaxy

paints me noble.   me who complains at the sough of his own heartbeat

me who speaks no tomorrow: fluent in today.

                                        me who likes *visit* and hates *stay*

my dwindling soul he went like hotcakes:

                                    me a success in the fine scant way

[you're thin again handsome. in our last]

you're thin again handsome.   in our last
hour together I'll be dabbing gravy off
your lip: stuck out.   an infirmary stoop

how can anything perplex us more than words
the pause in which we chew: parapraxia
I feed you lines.   you're a poor actor now
flubbing the bit part.   indignant us both

I'll want better for you than institutional
lunch in white paper.   pee stained underwear
a brief brief career as the delicious romantic lead

HIV?

g a t h e r   a t   t h e   r i v e r

"Mine is a world foregone though not yet ended,—

An imagined garden grey with sundered boughs

And broken branches, wistful and unmended,

And mist that is more constant than all vows"

—Hart Crane, "Postscript"

[always returning: holidays and burials. not every week]

always returning: holidays and burials.   not every week
has had its good friday.   except that lately latches
left unfastened for me.   biscuits rise in the piesafe
a dark suit smells less like mothballs: chrism

and condolences.   calendars come gaily from the florist
accounts receivable.   time and the supplier of easter
lilies: collusion.   we sit cozy in the parlor together
a cenotaph of cousinry.   unexpected guests do drop in

another place? time?

[not the treats of quince blossoms. in this rainy cycle the yards]

not the treats of quince blossoms.   in this rainy cycle the yards
are so much muck.   levees do not so much break as buckle

we would let the river baptize and afterward: so relieved of pressures
the earth could slide back into place: the houses slide back into houses
and the river a river perhaps: a change in its squiggle.   new foulard

we have been hit worse.   have let waters reserve the next county
as a chained hound.   a second coming.
                                         but with so few human casualties
the boating became a lark.   it wash away, we say, all this business

so we scrap:
                    this, the little nicknack we salvaged from the last great storm
a bauble floats up in the night: calls to us from among the darkest rushes

[autumn set us heavily to task: unrooted the dahlias]

autumn set us heavily to task: unrooted the dahlias
lay wrapped in the cellar.   cider pressing time.   grain milling
time to pick persimmons.   time to fix the leaky hayloft

slaughtering time.   rendering time.   time to put up chokecherries
take the woolens from the cedar chest: britches mending time
rabbit hunting time.   tallow candle dipping time.   soap making time

count the butter and egg money.   count the diapers in the wash
time to split wood and clean the flue.   time that the pesky swallows
in the chimney took their leave.   molasses cooking time

kids sent to glean the fields at dusk.   yams laid out to cure
and the last huckleberries balljarred in the larder.   corn husking time
clay dull red in sunlight crumbling: abundant the harvest and the tithe

[splat in the oatmeal: granddaddy facedown]

splat in the oatmeal: granddaddy facedown
disappeared the way a prize hog we were fond of

grandma got closer to: jeez.   not another
tale of armageddon.   she would beat us
at games of scrabble: biblical words latched
onto the vernacular.   challenges and curses

sometimes a prayer escapes: we are more
and less religious.   heaven hasn't swallowed her
up.   despite all our wishing it were so

[here comes the welcome wagon with its]

here comes the welcome wagon with its
melting pot: theory of assimilation

courteous gesture in swiss fondue
beware: the somber bass informs
beneath the overture brassly cordial

here come the long-handled forks
crusts of bread.   and such

[women stitching apron corners together. *neighborly*]

women stitching apron corners together.   *neighborly*
meaning free to walk beneath each other's clotheslines

parataxis of paperdoll mommies conjoin
cotton seraphim: tending the reckling brood

no jam jar is sacrosanct: hungry cubs
kiss their milk from the closest teat.   laundry

makes no clean sepiment.   between dwellings.   only arches
to parade through when called by name.   or aroma: fondly

this handsewn host descends with a tug
to wipe a smeared passel of lips: rinse

confection into the washbasin.   and would flock greyed
against the sky: winged and ready to take flight

[the future rose: an a-frame on the cumberland]

the future rose: an a-frame on the cumberland
pioneer stock tapering off.   balanced inclinations

fists forgot their hammers.   forearms atrophied
the frontier lay flattened against the roadway
wild things curled up: everyone was licked

cyclone improvements: the barn would not be replaced
nor would accents.   dulled in gentility: weakling wind

[splitzville for ann and mark: the tourniquet]

splitzville for ann and mark: the tourniquet
is cut loose.   no more cuts nor love bumps
cords around the neck.   bungee dives off the bed

he wears that bandage on his ring finger:
another woman stuffed in his drawers like a sock
he pulls her out at night: pummels her face
with those big lips.   puts out his flashlight

dreams are tight things with breasts.   triplets
pinch his cheeks.   when he feints to plant
a kiss he wakes: mouth full of chewed on sheets

skeleton of a story

42

[he achieved his escape: john wesley]

he achieved his escape: john wesley

from the slow assault of hands.   plunged

off the trestle neck and spine

snapping of kettle-fried chicken bones

a tablecloth laid over his remains

these collard.   this grits

the succulent drumsticks bearing witness

in a gathering of dixie-battered hens

[orphans of career day: the choicest lives already]

orphans of career day: the choicest lives already
appropriated.   sweatshops and gruel are beckoning

chairs and desks disappear one by one.   needle lifted
off the phonograph: all positions have been filled
they go forth on blistered feet.   vulgar talk

still the remembered tempo of music measures each step
a piper seems sweet.   the beat of drums and a line to enlist

[down with the chickenbumps you came: kerplunk]

down with the chickenbumps you came: kerplunk

spunky cannot play today.   at home with a case of school

work.   nothing on but election returns and black and

white ennui.   canned beanywienies are brother's fave

not yours: o for some frozen sympathy: dreamsicles

all the icecream they say you'll get when you get

what you got from that sibling.   the one you don't know

how to play with anymore: he's playing smear tackle

in the vacant lot.   while you hate his toy soldiers

bending their heads practically off: he'll be home late

slugging you in your "hey, that's my sore arm"

how brothers are buttholes: you write your theme for class

language used belies sentiment

45

[he imitates his wife: no young drop from the gap]

he imitates his wife: no young drop from the gap
of wishing between his thighs.   confiscating a dream
he kicks her out of bed: always stealing covers

couvade: a man receives congratulations of his friends
aping maternity: the spurious faucet of his chest
suckles plastic dolls.   a practice labor
quivers across his tummy.   contractions

rouse him in the night.   she can bear the pain
and bears away.   as if no more a burden than his touch

See 4.2

46

[dearest perdition. your sweet peach kisses lost]

> "If we manage to suppress the Oedipus complex and marriage,
> what would be left for us to tell?"
> —Roland Barthes

dearest perdition.   your sweet peach kisses lost
their true asperity: echolalia.   we go drunk
through another rehearsal: one another's guests

and are not bellicose.   I don't seem oedipusblind
nor you medeamad: caesura in the classical text
book case.   taciturn: we hold each other's breath

e.e. cummings and a fever but...

a puzzle

[baby's on a pallet. in the screenporch you iron]

baby's on a pallet.　in the screenporch you iron
bluing and starching to temporary perfection:　fabrication
this acreage stales you in its chestnuts.　termagant
you are beyond your dolly expectations:　saddled

you have a man with the talent to ted manure.　ripening
bark and worm castings scatter about your feet:　flinch
hard to make it away.　the soiled dukes of his hands:
slops of his meals:　tugging of his husbandry at your hem

[sonnet]

a song of the cinema /

morsels of my lifeswork: the story of a professional party hostess
I call this film "edge that can't know what I'm taking with me"
familiar and not shakespiliar.   think eurythmics think newamericanwriting   *look up*

a nice mix of plights and music.   boomerang boy and disco dollies
I call this film "edge of a terrific current issue full of vice"
going to have witchdoctors in it.   evil barbies.   caymans and gators

written in an enjoyable present: continuous.   an unresolved work
I think I'll call it "edge literate and fresh and ugly."   and "suitable?"
most of the shooting to be done in okinawa, okeechobee and omaha

most of the shooting nightlit super8 and under extreme conditions
roll credits:
           I call this film "edge that can't imagine how, given the situation"
suppose I'll be shopping for boots or intoxicants.   props and settings

if you get my machine I'm on location: hazy hot humid.
                                         the far reaches
not to live, mind you.
              to wrap up "edge where headed the winging cranes"

[the rain deliberately falls: as an older boy's hand]

the rain deliberately falls: as an older boy's hand

would drop into my lap.   I did like the wet

let trickle against my soft: disturbingly

precious the way I caught it.   mouth stretched wide

now I rush to cover up.   even the telling

clouds: frightening.   I wear my slicker outside

don't want to catch my death: feel its grip

connectedness

(Tea.)

[old age keeps its reservation. nostalgia]

old age keeps its reservation.   nostalgia
is best thought to be past: lap trays
pop up startlingly.   familiar playgrounds

spoon: a blunt instrument.   purees
and porridges stir the weak.   recall
faltering vision seeks some recognizable form

we know a bib.   remember a tune
curse the mushy texture of dear friends

with teeth wedded to sink: as in "under the"
distinction softens into pablum.   dissolves

reversability

i n   t h e   m i d d l e   o f   t h e   a i r

"first we were darkness, then we were galaxies,

traveling too fast too far for me to call

throughout all that space goodbye

my twin my half

of the light, goodbye my little bit famous—"

—Brenda Hillman, "Time Zone"

[we all carry signs of our obsessions]

we all carry signs of our obsessions
you your needletracks.   I my stretchmarks

no sleuth need rummage our files   *post self-disclosure*

I flatten my belly: a hamlet ballerina
o that this tutu of solid flesh.   melt

[third-world hunger strikes you. midtown bus]

a song of the virus

third-world hunger strikes you.   midtown bus
passion settles in the tenderloin.   ravenous

you thrive on the gaunt busboy: chops
respond pavlovian to the tinkling of poverty

your wallet can afford you. some protection
an allowance to rut among the cheaper cuts
a scavenger: you feed off them.   skinny skinny legs

[in the new genesis: a part of his skeleton became me. shaped me]

in the new genesis: a part of his skeleton became me.   shaped me

me as womb trembles forth.   me wifeless with 300,000 retro sons

me of no husband girdled and they to no spouse parceled:

                                                    bits of gopherwood

theogony: must my skull be hut for them all?

                                        at night the anvils sing *bingbong*

them kids is pounding out more kids.   listen: dna clinks its chainmail

old soldier my body cannot hold: rickety ark.

                                    no more doves can land here

time → bleeding
history

female voice

[you don't have syphilis. the doctor says]

you don't have syphilis.   the doctor says

you don't have hepatitis.   he says

you aren't diabetic.   the doctor says

cholesterol level normal.   blood pressure

good.   he says you've got great reflexes

the doctor says these things.   he's the doctor

he says I *do* have a bit of bad news.   he says

just like that: I *do* have a bit of bad news

not a *real* doctor remember: a physician's *assistant*

[handwritten: most accessible, more polite]

[because as lives are aching I am lucky: a poisonal cup]

because as lives are aching I am lucky: a poisonal cup

I ingest pill after mastodon pill.   after I have abdominal pains

headaches, skin aches, bone aches, the drowse and nausea

no matter pill or bitter pill.   but no milk rare and no meat fat

nor oysters: doctor's orders.   my mouth going blind over and over

nothing spicy or sharp.   forgetting I eat my hair.   I say our dear lord:

losing myself in public.   seems sunday loves my mouth and music

we supper [me and poison].   together we bath [poison and me].

we live together difficultly.   and fairly normal:

                              doing all the poisoning myself

myself.   need no wine to sanctify.   as of the right now I am lucky:

need no litter bearer.   children undigested I am able to throw back up

[in the course of travel: strychnine every few hours. some italian art]

in the course of travel: strychnine every few hours.   some italian art
and trees yes pretty but it's the normal routine.   well, "normal routine"

you easterners: your maple trees.   you have your maple trees.

                                                       your nation
and me my eyes bugging late and funny:

                                      scrub compared to the maple trees

every few hours flash fevers.   every few and I'd be small.   a bit nervous
the evening distended as a bad patella: oh my knee.   and I had to pee

virtually every few minutes.   someone catches me under the maple trees
taken out of context: like a trip on a yacht or dying.com.

                                       I would not go

there: among the trees I stood almost grand and well.

                                       with my own nuts
my own birdlike nuts.   my own startled happiness at the slightest breeze

—for Tom Thompson

[when dementia begins:

        almost makes sense like hamburger translations]

when dementia begins: almost makes sense like hamburger translations

or the poems the body writes in its dysentery:

                      explosions at either end and vile

my mind has many homes these days.   I have seen much of kitchen tile

much of the great round bowls.

               in doorways I lose the heartbeat of decisions

me is no comfort place to be these days.

                  hang teeth and smiles in the windows

and fiddle fiddle with the thermostat.

             but the mind don't stay: away to the mall

let the lookylous look: rupt rush re so re bo re we re wa re yo reat reali reall

see streets of a lost city.

          the lights beyond keep blinking how yet how yet hows

[cherry elixir: the first medication. so mary poppins]

cherry elixir: the first medication.   so mary poppins
a chance to acclimate: an infant dose.   a baby step
supplanting pneumonia half a teaspoon at a time

until the tablet can be tolerated.   with adult strength
my throat constricts around unspeckled eggs: rosy boa

everybody talks about the cocktail: sounds delicious
I think in jello flavors.   picturing umbrellas in tall glass
the cocktail up.   the cocktail over.   straws and serviettes

not a steel spansule.   not a fistful of bloated tictacs.   no burn
in the bowels the belly & the mouth.   want my goddamn cocktail

ABOUT THE AUTHOR

D. A. Powell, author of *tea*, (Wesleyan, 1998), has received awards from the Academy of American Poets and the James Michener Foundation. He currently resides in San Francisco, where he has taught at San Francisco State University and the University of San Francisco.

LIBRARY OF CONGRESS CATALOGING-IN-PUBLICATION DATA

Powell, D. A.

Lunch / by D. A. Powell.

    p. cm. — (Wesleyan poetry)

ISBN 0–8195–6426–5 (cl : alk. paper)   ISBN 0–8195–6427–3 (pa : alk. paper).

I. Title.   II. Series.

PS3566.O828T4   2000

811'.54—dc21   97–44599